Editorial Project Manager
Mara Ellen Guckian

Managing Editors
Karen J. Goldfluss, M.S. Ed.
Ina Massler Levin, M. A.

Art Coordinator
Renée Christine Yates

Illustrator
Kevin McCarthy

Cover Artist
Denise Bauer

Art Production Manager
Kevin Barnes

Imaging
Rosa C. See

Publisher
Mary D. Smith, M.S. Ed.

Full-Color

Reading Games

Grades Pre·K–K

- Letter Recognition
- Initial Consonant Sounds
- Ending Sounds

Authors

Bridget Kilroy Hoffman

Julie R. Mauer, M.A.

Teacher Created Resources, Inc.
6421 Industry Way
Westminster, CA 92683
www.teachercreated.com
ISBN-1-4206-3120-9
©2006 Teacher Created Resources, Inc.
Made in U.S.A.

Table of Contents

Introduction 3

Helpful Hints 4

Game Assembly and Storage 4

Outrageous Ocean *(Letter Recognition)*

Sammy Sea Otter 5

Otto Octopus 19

A Sea of Seahorses 33

Whale Watching 47

Playful Pets *(Initial Consonant Sounds)*

Flashy Fish 61

Happy Hamsters 75

Baby Birds 89

Kitten Kingdom 103

Friendly Farms *(Ending Sounds)*

Cowboy in the Cornfield 117

Hay Rack Ride 131

Barnyard Buddies 145

Curly the Cow 159

Parent Letter 173

Instructions for Family Fun Reading Games 174

Game Labels 175

Picture Card Identification Key 176

Introduction

Full-Color Reading Games is a collection of brightly illustrated board games. The games offer young learners the necessary practice for building important reading skills. Reading games help students make associations between letters and sounds. *Full-Color Reading Games* is designed for the creative pre-kindergarten or kindergarten teacher who strives to provide his/her students with more than just worksheets for practice and review. While worksheet-based resource books are easy to reproduce and implement in a classroom, they do not spark curiosity or spark interest with young learners. These exciting skill-building games serve as a powerful and playful alternative to worksheets. Use *Full-Color Reading Games* to facilitate the teaching of fundamental phonics skills and to nurture a child's early reading development.

This valuable teacher resource is organized by theme and concept. Each attractive board game captures the attention of young learners, is relevant to their interests, and develops teamwork. The whole group works together to successfully complete the game. The concepts covered are specifically designed for use with students in the beginning stages of the reading process. Through play, children will practice the following skills:

- Recognize uppercase letters
- Recognize lowercase letters
- Identify partner letters by matching upper and lowercase letters
- Associate sounds with letters
- Identify initial consonant sounds of pictures
- Match consonant sounds to the appropriate letters in the initial position
- Identify ending sounds of pictures
- Match consonant sounds to the appropriate letters in the ending position
- Understand the difference between letter names and letter sounds.

These colorful reading games are easy to assemble. Just follow the directions outlined in the Preparation section for each game to create great games that can be used in the classroom in a matter of minutes. You determine how your students will use the games, be it with partners, in small groups, as center activities, one-on-one for student assessment, or as take-home practice for family fun. Emphasize with the students that the goal is to work together to complete the game boards. (Everybody wins.)

Any way you choose to use them, *Full-Color Reading Games* will provide young learners with the ability to link sounds to specific letters and master basic reading skills. Incorporate these games into your existing curriculum or share them with parents to use at home. You will be rewarded as your students begin the process of becoming successful lifelong readers.

Helpful Hints

The games in *Full-Color Reading Games* provide teachers with multiple options for use in the classroom. The games encourage teamwork. Everyone succeeds when the game is finished.

- *Small group:* Have two, three, or four students play together or with the teacher.
- *Partners:* Allow two students to play together.
- *Center activities:* Place the games in a reading center to reinforce whole-group reading instruction.
- *Practice and review:* Use all four games about a particular concept with as many as 16 students at the same time.
- *Individual assessment:* Have one student complete a game independently; then, check the game to assess student progress.
- *Family fun:* Send the game home with students for further enhancement of reading skills.

The directions for each of the games in a theme are similar. When you introduce one game in the set, students can transition easily to the other games. Students can even teach other students how to play.

> *Note:* It is important to review each set of picture cards before playing a game. Some pictures could be interpreted differently. (Examples—block/cube, tub/bathtub, zig zag/squiggle)

Game Assembly and Storage

All of the games in *Full-Color Reading Games* are easy to assemble. Below are just a few suggestions on how to prepare and store them.

- Using a color photocopy machine, copy the games and keep the original book as your master, or dismantle the entire book by separating the pages on the perforated lines and copy the direction cards and manipulative pages for future reference. Create each game as outlined in the Preparation section of the directions card.
- Assemble the full-color game board by taping the two pages together. Mount the game board on a 12" x 18" piece of construction paper, oak tag, poster board, or file folder. Laminate for durability.
- Laminate and cut out all necessary game pieces such as flashcards, cover up cards, and directions cards. The cover up cards for each game may be cut out as cards or on the picture outline. (Note: Four additional cover up cards are provided for each game.)
- Store flashcards, cover up cards and direction cards in resealable snack bags. Label each bag with the game name label provided in the back of this book (page 175), and attach each bag of game pieces to its game board.
- Organize the entire collection of board games in plastic file boxes, durable magazine/book holders, desktop file holders, or see-through plastic envelopes with button-and-string fasteners or Velcro® closures.

Sammy Sea Otter

Letter Recognition

Objective: To recognize and match uppercase and lowercase letters.

Preparation

1. Assemble and laminate the Sammy Sea Otter Game Board (pages 8 and 9).

2. Laminate and cut out the Sammy Sea Otter Lowercase Letter Cards (pages 11, 13, and 15).

3. Laminate and cut out the Bubble Cover Ups (page 17).

4. Laminate the Sammy Sea Otter Directions Card (page 5).

5. Store the Sammy Sea Otter Lowercase Letter Cards and Bubble Cover Ups in a resealable snack bag. Label the bag with the game name label (page 175).

6. See page 176 for the correct picture card names.

Sammy Sea Otter Directions

Materials

- Sammy Sea Otter Game Board
- Sammy Sea Otter Lowercase Letter Cards
- Bubble Cover Ups

How to Play the Game

2–4 players

1. Shuffle the lowercase letter cards and place them facedown beside the Sammy Sea Otter Game Board.

2. Divide the Bubble Cover Ups among the players.

3. Take turns drawing a lowercase letter card and covering the matching uppercase letter on the game board with a cover up.

4. Continue taking turns until all the uppercase letters on the Sammy Sea Otter Game Board have been covered.

a   b   c

d   e   f

g   h   i

Sammy Sea Otter

Sammy Sea Otter

Sammy Sea Otter

Sammy Sea Otter

Sammy Sea Otter

Sammy Sea Otter

Sammy Sea Otter

Sammy Sea Otter

Sammy Sea Otter

j

k

l

m

n

o

p

q

r

Sammy Sea Otter

Sammy

Sea

Otter

Sammy

Sea

Otter

Sammy

Sea

Otter

Sammy

Sea

Otter

Sammy

Sea

Otter

Sammy

Sea

Otter

Sammy

Sea

Otter

Sammy

Sea

Otter

Sammy

Sea

Otter

s

t

<u>u</u>

v

w

x

y

z

Sammy Sea Otter

Sammy
Sea
Otter

Sammy
Sea
Otter

Sammy
Sea
Otter

Sammy
Sea
Otter

Sammy
Sea
Otter

Sammy
Sea
Otter

Sammy
Sea
Otter

Sammy
Sea
Otter

Sammy
Sea
Otter

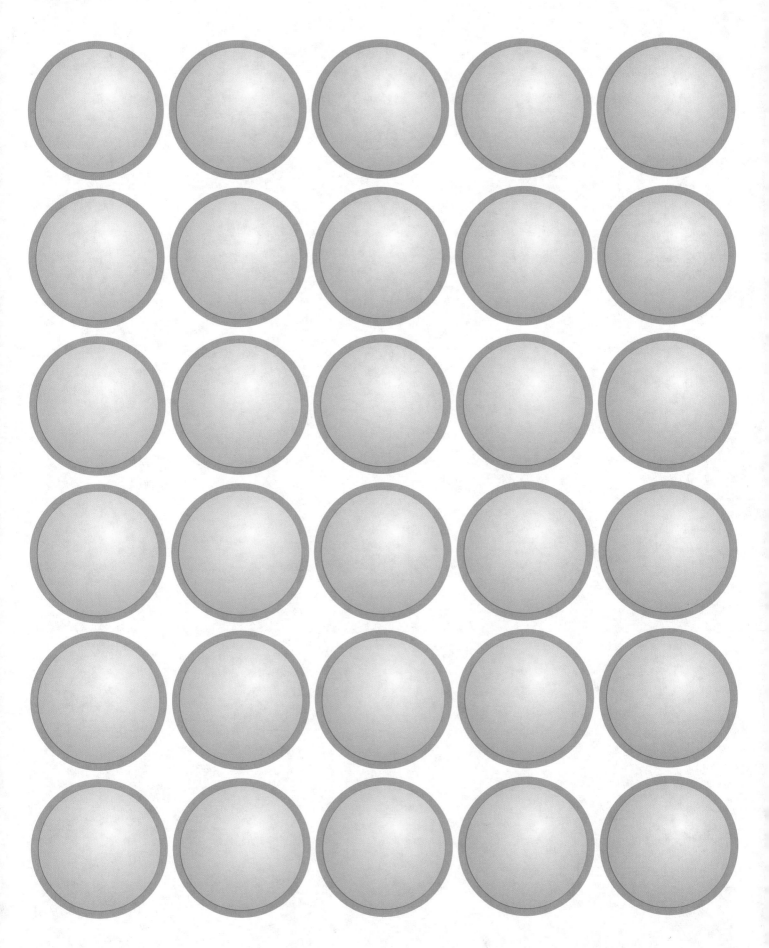

Otto Octopus

Letter Recognition

Objective: To recognize and match uppercase and lowercase letters.

Preparation

1. Assemble and laminate the Otto Octopus Game Board (pages 22 and 23).

2. Laminate and cut out the Otto Octopus Uppercase Letter Cards (pages 25, 27 and 29).

3. Laminate and cut out the Spot Cover Ups (page 31).

4. Laminate the Otto Octopus Directions Card (page 19).

5. Store the Otto Octopus Uppercase Letter Cards and Spot Cover Ups in a resealable snack bag. Label the bag with the game name label (page 175).

6. See page 176 for the correct picture card names.

Otto Octopus Directions

Materials

- Otto Octopus Game Board
- Otto Octopus Uppercase Letter Cards
- Spot Cover Ups

How to Play the Game

2–4 players

1. Shuffle the uppercase letter cards and place them facedown beside the Otto Octopus Game Board.

2. Divide the different-colored Spot Cover Ups among the players.

3. Take turns drawing an uppercase letter card and covering the matching lowercase letter on the game board with a cover up.

4. Continue taking turns until all the lowercase letters on the Otto Octopus Game Board have been covered.

A   B   C

D   E   F

G   H   I

Otto Octopus

Otto
Octopus

Otto
Octopus

Otto
Octopus

Otto
Octopus

Otto
Octopus

Otto
Octopus

Otto
Octopus

Otto
Octopus

Otto
Octopus

J   K   L

M   N   O

P   Q   R

Otto Octopus

Otto
Octopus

Otto
Octopus

Otto
Octopus

Otto
Octopus

Otto
Octopus

Otto
Octopus

Otto
Octopus

Otto
Octopus

Otto
Octopus

S   T   U

V   W   X

Y   Z

Otto
Octopus

Otto
Octopus

Otto
Octopus

Otto
Octopus

Otto
Octopus

Otto
Octopus

Otto
Octopus

Otto
Octopus

Otto
Octopus

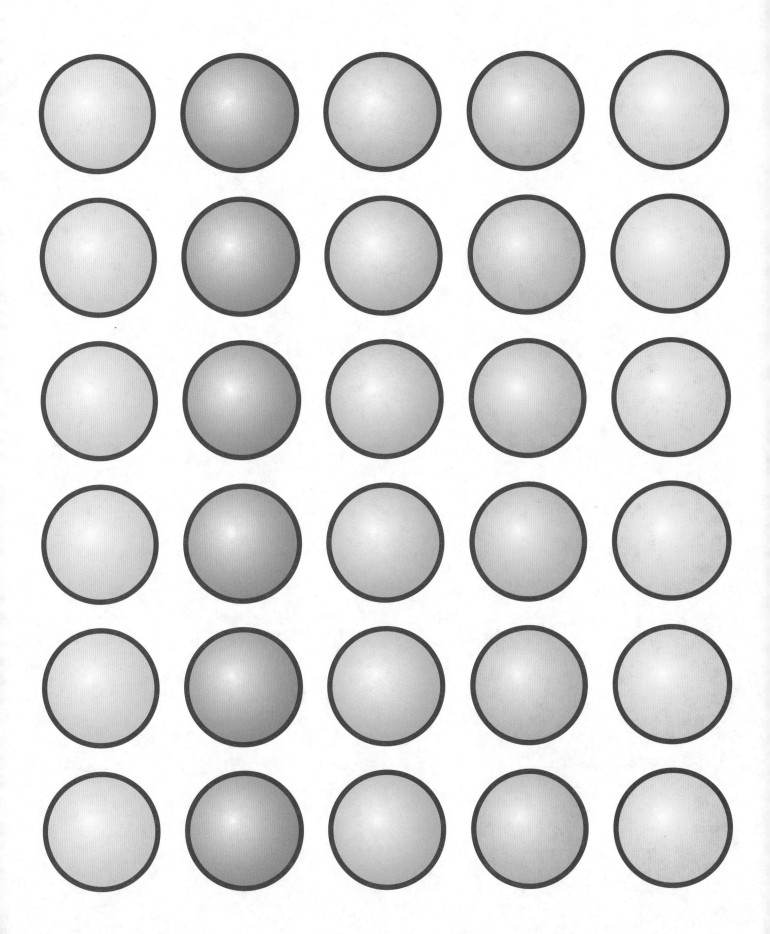

A Sea of Seahorses

Letter Recognition

Objective: To recognize and match uppercase and lowercase letters.

Preparation

1. Assemble and laminate the A Sea of Seahorses Game Board (pages 36 and 37).

2. Laminate and cut out the A Sea of Seahorses Lowercase Letter Cards (pages 39, 41, and 43).

3. Laminate and cut out the Seahorse Cover Ups (page 45).

4. Laminate the A Sea of Seahorses Directions Card (page 33).

5. Store the A Sea of Seahorses Lowercase Letter Cards and Seahorse Cover Ups in a resealable snack bag. Label the bag with the game name label (page 175).

6. See page 176 for the correct picture card names.

A Sea of Seahorses Directions

Materials

- A Sea of Seahorses Game Board
- A Sea of Seahorses Lowercase Letter Cards
- Seahorse Cover Ups

How to Play the Game

2–4 players

1. Shuffle the lowercase letter cards and place them facedown beside the A Sea of Seahorses Game Board.

2. Divide the Seahorse Cover Ups among the players.

3. Take turns drawing a lowercase letter card and covering the matching uppercase letter on the game board with a cover up.

4. Continue taking turns until all the uppercase letters on the A Sea of Seahorses Game Board have been covered.

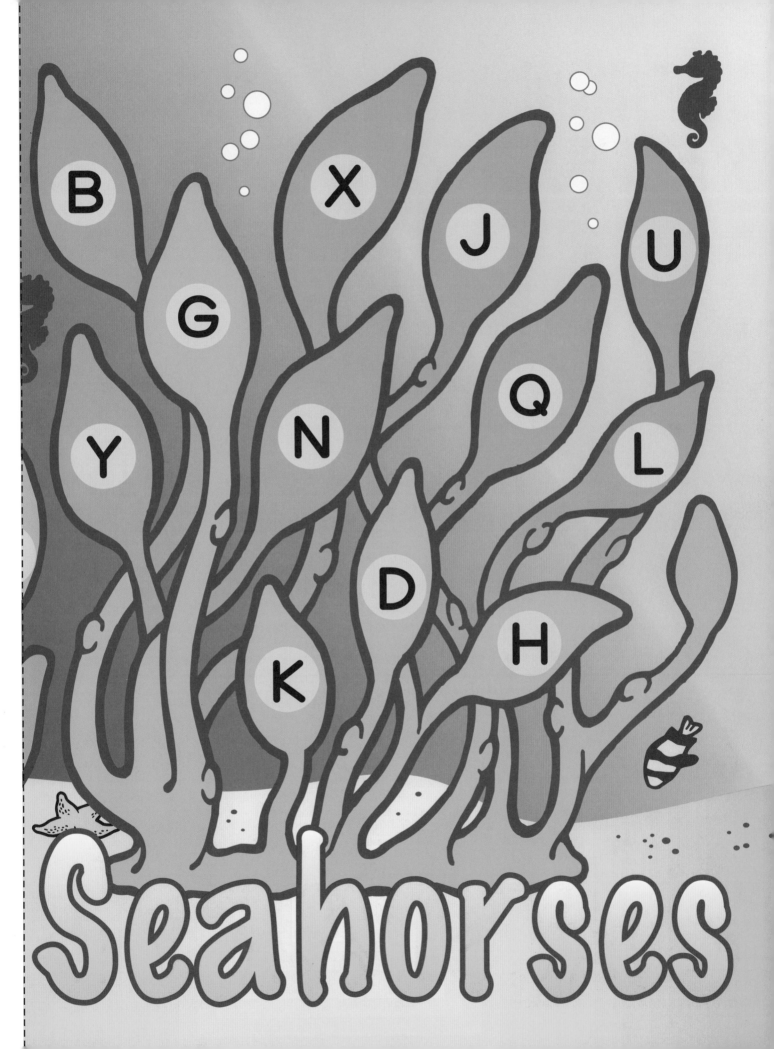

a b c

d e f

g h i

A Sea of Seahorses

A Sea of Seahorses

A Sea of Seahorses

A Sea of Seahorses

A Sea of Seahorses

A Sea of Seahorses

A Sea of Seahorses

A Sea of Seahorses

A Sea of Seahorses

A Sea of Seahorses

j　　k　　l

m　　n　　o

p　　q　　r

A Sea of Seahorses

A Sea of Seahorses	A Sea of Seahorses	A Sea of Seahorses
A Sea of Seahorses	A Sea of Seahorses	A Sea of Seahorses
A Sea of Seahorses	A Sea of Seahorses	A Sea of Seahorses

s

t

u

v

w

x

y

z

A Sea of Seahorses

A Sea of Seahorses

A Sea of Seahorses

A Sea of Seahorses

A Sea of Seahorses

A Sea of Seahorses

A Sea of Seahorses

A Sea of Seahorses

A Sea of Seahorses

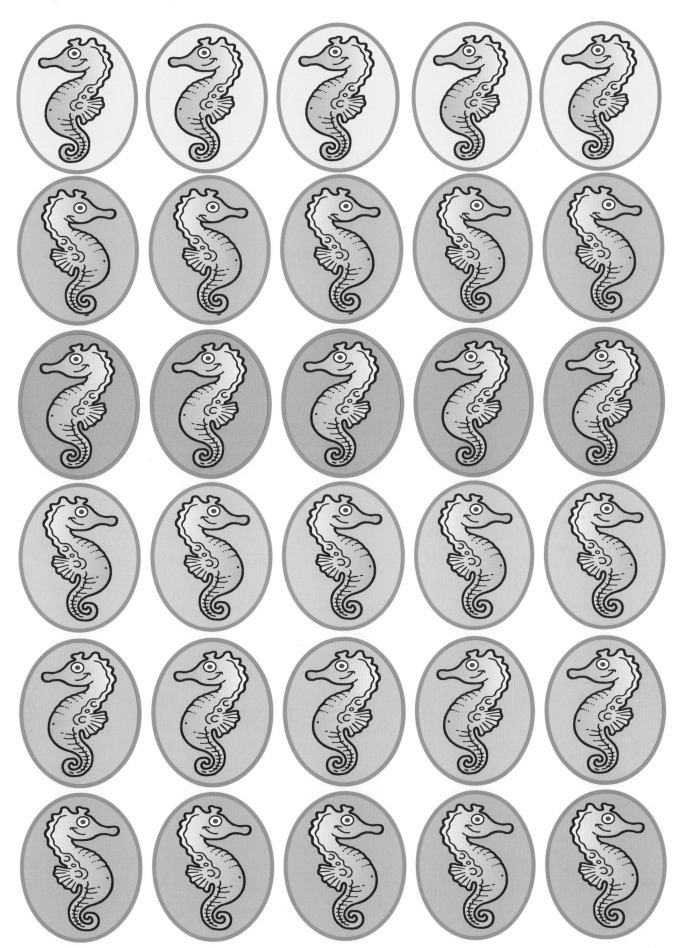

Whale Watching

Letter Recognition

Objective: To recognize and match uppercase and lowercase letters.

Preparation

1. Assemble and laminate the Whale Watching Game Board (pages 50 and 51).

2. Laminate and cut out the Whale Watching Uppercase Letter Cards (pages 53, 55, and 57).

3. Laminate and cut out the Barnacle Cover Ups (page 59).

4. Laminate the Whale Watching Directions Card (page 47).

5. Store the Whale Watching Uppercase Letter Cards and Barnacle Cover Ups in a resealable snack bag. Label the bag with the game name label (page 175).

6. See page 176 for the correct picture card names.

Whale Watching Directions

Materials

- Whale Watching Game Board
- Whale Watching Uppercase Letter Cards
- Barnacle Cover Ups

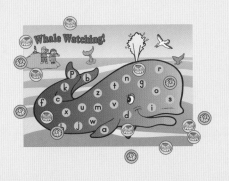

How to Play the Game

2–4 players

1. Shuffle the uppercase letter cards and place them facedown beside the Whale Watching Game Board.

2. Divide the Barnacle Cover Ups among the players.

3. Take turns drawing an uppercase letter card and covering the matching lowercase letter on the game board with a cover up.

4. Continue taking turns until all the lowercase letters on the Whale Watching Game Board have been covered.

49

Whale Watching

A   B   C

D   E   F

G   H   I

Whale Watching

Whale   Whale   Whale
Watching   Watching   Watching

Whale   Whale   Whale
Watching   Watching   Watching

Whale   Whale   Whale
Watching   Watching   Watching

©Teacher Created Resources, Inc.

J K L

M N O

P Q R

Whale Watching

Whale
Watching

Whale
Watching

Whale
Watching

Whale
Watching

Whale
Watching

Whale
Watching

Whale
Watching

Whale
Watching

Whale
Watching

S   T   U

V   W   X

Y   Z

Whale Watching

Whale
Watching

Whale
Watching

Whale
Watching

Whale
Watching

Whale
Watching

Whale
Watching

Whale
Watching

Whale
Watching

Whale
Watching

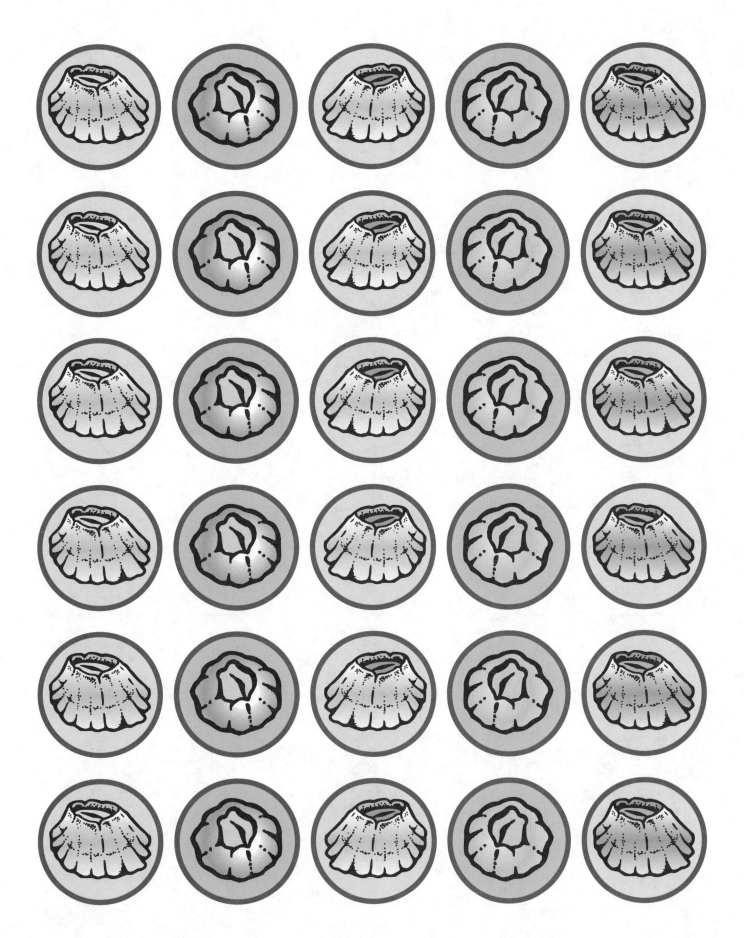

Flashy Fish

Initial Consonant Sounds

Objective: To identify initial consonant sounds of pictures and match to appropriate consonant letters.

Preparation

1. Assemble and laminate the Flashy Fish Game Board (pages 64 and 65).

2. Laminate and cut out the Flashy Fish Initial Consonant Sound Picture Cards (pages 67, 69, and 71).

3. Laminate and cut out the Fish Cover Ups (page 73).

4. Laminate the Flashy Fish Directions Card (page 61).

5. Store the Flashy Fish Initial Consonant Sound Picture Cards and Fish Cover Ups in a resealable snack bag. Label the bag with the game name label (page 175).

6. See page 176 for the correct picture card names.

Flashy Fish Directions

Materials

- Flashy Fish Game Board
- Flashy Fish Initial Consonant Sound Picture Cards
- Fish Cover Ups

How to Play the Game

2–4 players

1. Shuffle the initial consonant sound picture cards and place them facedown beside the Flashy Fish Game Board.

2. Divide the Fish Cover Ups among the players.

3. Take turns drawing an initial consonant sound picture card and covering the matching consonant letter on the game board with a cover up.

4. Continue taking turns until all the consonant letters on the Flashy Fish Game Board have been covered.

Flash!

j h y g w b s n m f

Flashy
Fish

Flashy
Fish

Flashy
Fish

Flashy
Fish

Flashy
Fish

Flashy
Fish

Flashy
Fish

Flashy
Fish

Initial Consonant Sound Picture Cards

Flashy
Fish

Flashy
Fish

Flashy
Fish

Flashy
Fish

Flashy
Fish

Flashy
Fish

Initial Consonant Sound Picture Cards

Flashy
Fish

Flashy
Fish

Flashy
Fish

Flashy
Fish

Flashy
Fish

Flashy
Fish

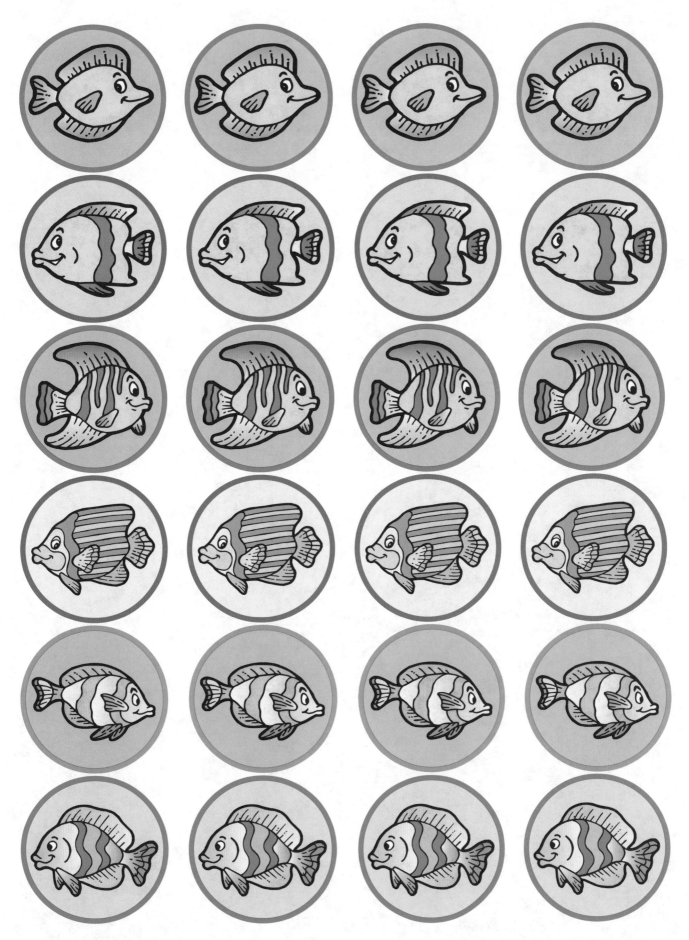

Happy Hamsters

Initial Consonant Sounds

Objective: To identify initial consonant sounds of pictures and match to appropriate consonant letters.

Preparation

1. Assemble and laminate the Happy Hamsters Game Board (pages 78 and 79).

2. Laminate and cut out the Happy Hamsters Initial Consonant Sound Picture Cards (pages 81, 83, and 85).

3. Laminate and cut out the Hamster Cover Ups (page 87).

4. Laminate the Happy Hamsters Directions Card (page 75).

5. Store the Happy Hamsters Initial Consonant Sound Picture Cards and Hamster Cover Ups in a resealable snack bag. Label the bag with the game name label (page 175).

6. See page 176 for the correct picture card names.

Happy Hamsters Directions

Materials

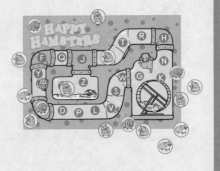

- Happy Hamsters Game Board
- Happy Hamsters Initial Consonant Sound Picture Cards
- Hamster Cover Ups

How to Play the Game

2–4 players

1. Shuffle the initial consonant sound picture cards and place them facedown beside the Happy Hamsters Game Board.

2. Divide the Hamster Cover Ups among the players.

3. Take turns drawing an initial consonant sound picture card and covering the matching consonant letter on the game board with a cover up.

4. Continue taking turns until all the consonant letters on the Happy Hamsters Game Board have been covered.

 #3120 Full-Color Reading Games Pre K–K

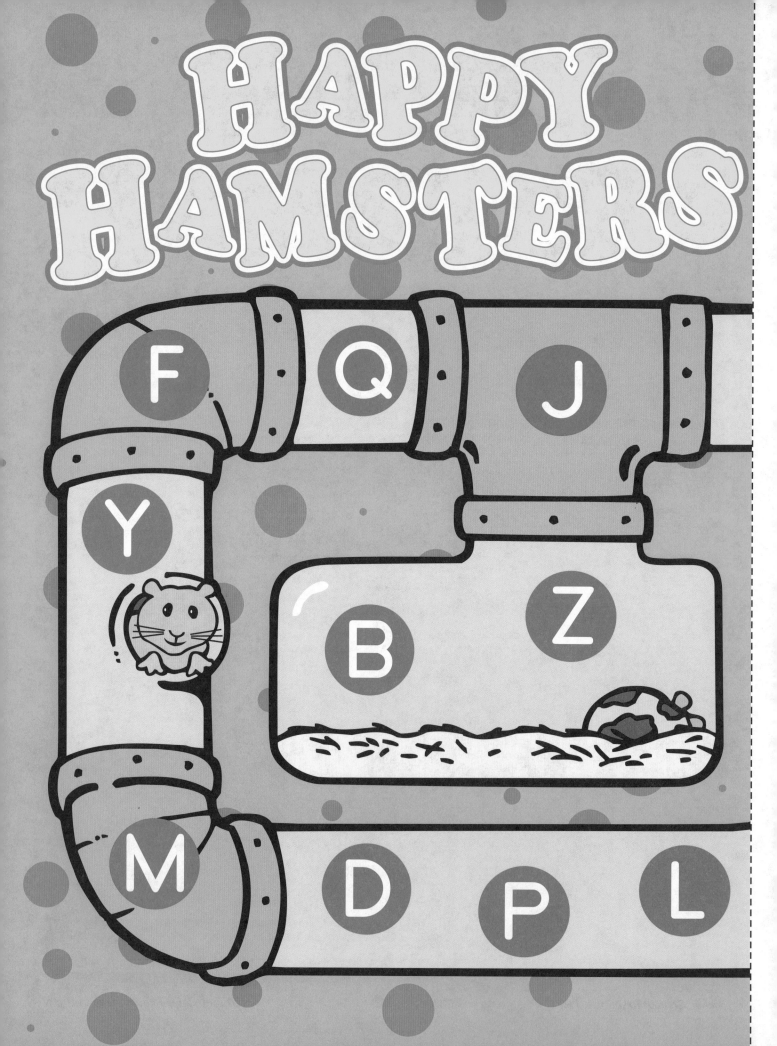

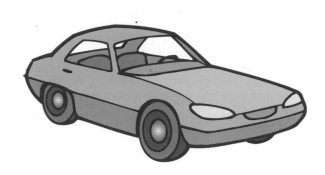

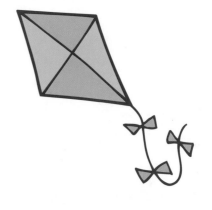

Initial Consonant Sound Picture Cards

Happy
Hamsters

Happy
Hamsters

Happy
Hamsters

Happy
Hamsters

Happy
Hamsters

Happy
Hamsters

Happy
Hamsters

Happy
Hamsters

Initial Consonant Sound Picture Cards

Happy
Hamsters

Happy
Hamsters

Happy
Hamsters

Happy
Hamsters

Happy
Hamsters

Happy
Hamsters

#3120 Full-Color Reading Games Pre K–K

Happy
Hamsters

Happy
Hamsters

Happy
Hamsters

Happy
Hamsters

Happy
Hamsters

Happy
Hamsters

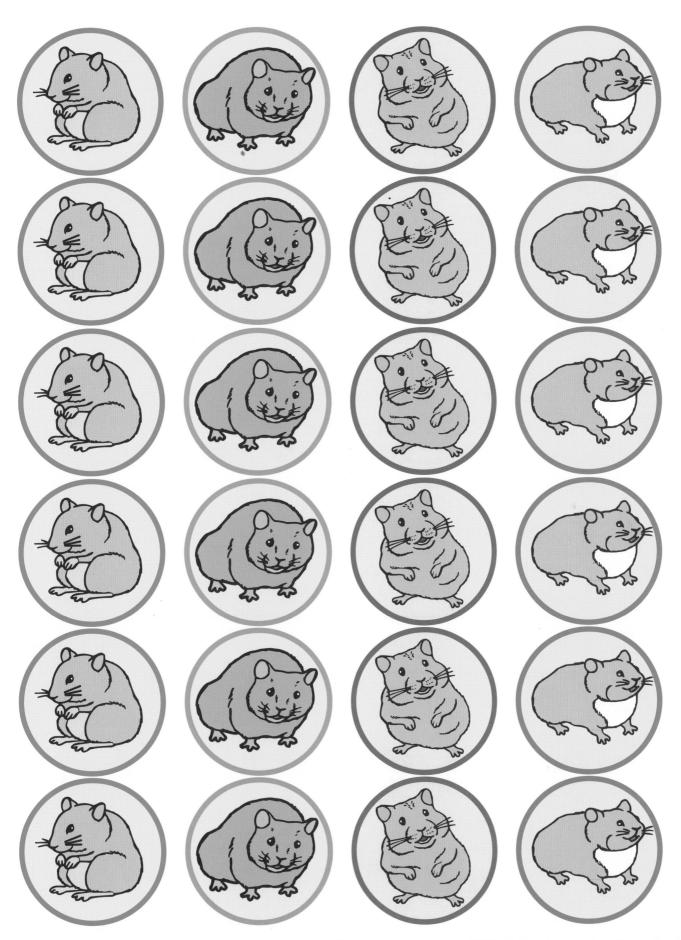

Baby Birds

Initial Consonant Sounds

Objective: To identify initial consonant sounds of pictures and match to appropriate consonant letters.

Preparation

1. Assemble and laminate the Baby Birds Game Board (pages 92 and 93).

2. Laminate and cut out the Baby Birds Initial Consonant Sound Picture Cards (pages 95, 97, and 99).

3. Laminate and cut out the Bird Cover Ups (page 101).

4. Laminate the Baby Birds Directions Card (page 89).

5. Store the Baby Birds Initial Consonant Sound Picture Cards and Bird Cover Ups in a resealable snack bag. Label the bag with the game name label (page 175).

6. See page 176 for the correct picture card names.

Baby Birds Directions

Materials

- Baby Birds Game Board
- Baby Birds Initial Consonant Sound Picture Cards
- Bird Cover Ups

How to Play the Game

2–4 players

1. Shuffle the initial consonant sound picture cards and place them facedown beside the Baby Birds Game Board.

2. Divide the Bird Cover Ups among the players.

3. Take turns drawing an initial consonant sound picture card and covering the matching consonant letter on the game board with a cover up.

4. Continue taking turns until all the consonant letters on the Baby Birds Game Board have been covered.

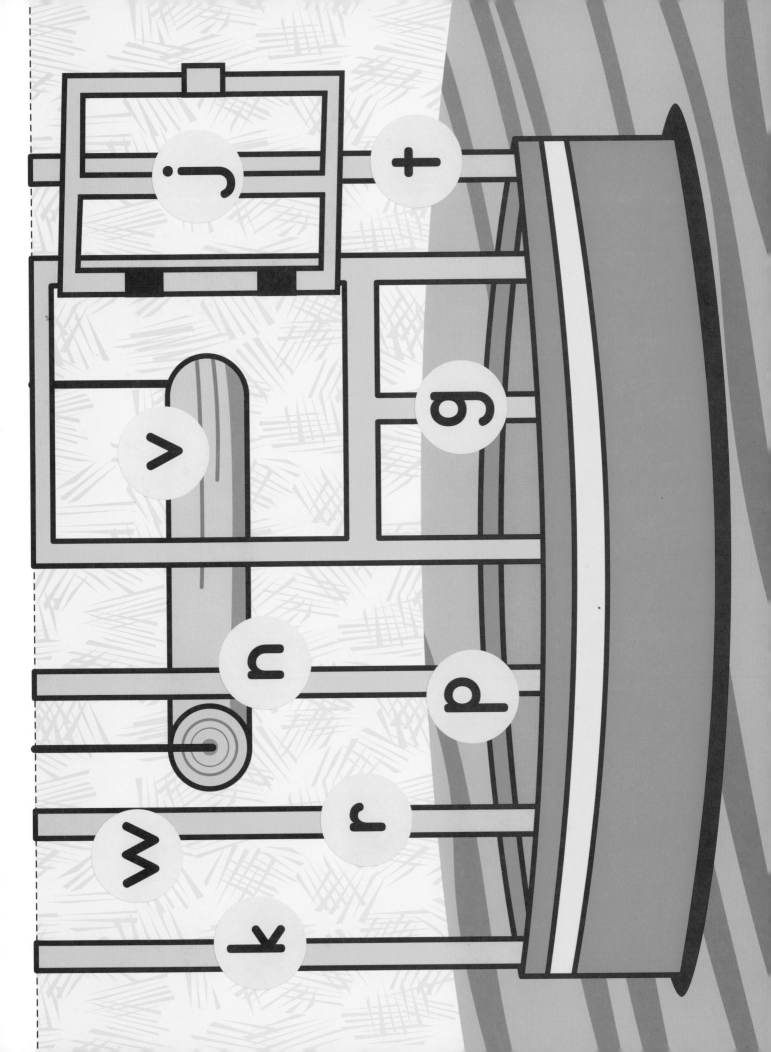

Initial Consonant Sound Picture Cards

Baby
Birds

Baby
Birds

Baby
Birds

Baby
Birds

Baby
Birds

Baby
Birds

Baby
Birds

Baby
Birds

Initial Consonant Sound Picture Cards

Baby Birds

Baby Birds

Baby Birds

Baby Birds

Baby Birds

Baby Birds

Baby
Birds

Baby
Birds

Baby
Birds

Baby
Birds

Baby
Birds

Baby
Birds

Kitten Kingdom

Initial Consonant Sounds

Objective: To identify initial consonant sounds of pictures and match to appropriate consonant letters.

Preparation

1. Assemble and laminate the Kitten Kingdom Game Board (pages 106 and 107).

2. Laminate and cut out the Kitten Kingdom Initial Consonant Sound Picture Cards (pages 109, 111, and 113).

3. Laminate and cut out the Paw Print Cover Ups (page 115).

4. Laminate the Kitten Kingdom Directions Card (page 103).

5. Store the Kitten Kingdom Initial Consonant Sound Picture Cards and Paw Print Cover Ups in a resealable snack bag. Label the bag with the game name label (page 175).

6. See page 176 for the correct picture card names.

Kitten Kingdom Directions

Materials

- Kitten Kingdom Game Board
- Kitten Kingdom Initial Consonant Sound Picture Cards
- Paw Print Cover Ups

How to Play the Game

2–4 players

1. Shuffle the initial consonant sound picture cards and place them facedown beside the Kitten Kingdom Game Board.

2. Divide the Paw Print Cover Ups among the players.

3. Take turns drawing an initial consonant sound picture card and covering the matching consonant letter on the game board with a cover up.

4. Continue taking turns until all the consonant letters on the Kitten Kingdom Game Board have been covered.

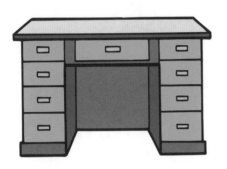

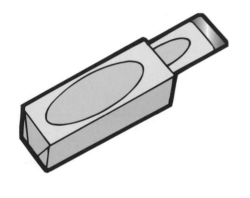

Initial Consonant Sound Picture Cards

Kitten
Kingdom

Kitten
Kingdom

Kitten
Kingdom

Kitten
Kingdom

Kitten
Kingdom

Kitten
Kingdom

Kitten
Kingdom

Kitten
Kingdom

Initial Consonant Sound Picture Cards

Kitten

Kingdom

Kitten

Kingdom

Kitten

Kingdom

Kitten

Kingdom

Kitten

Kingdom

Kitten

Kingdom

Kitten
Kingdom

Kitten
Kingdom

Kitten
Kingdom

Kitten
Kingdom

Kitten
Kingdom

Kitten
Kingdom

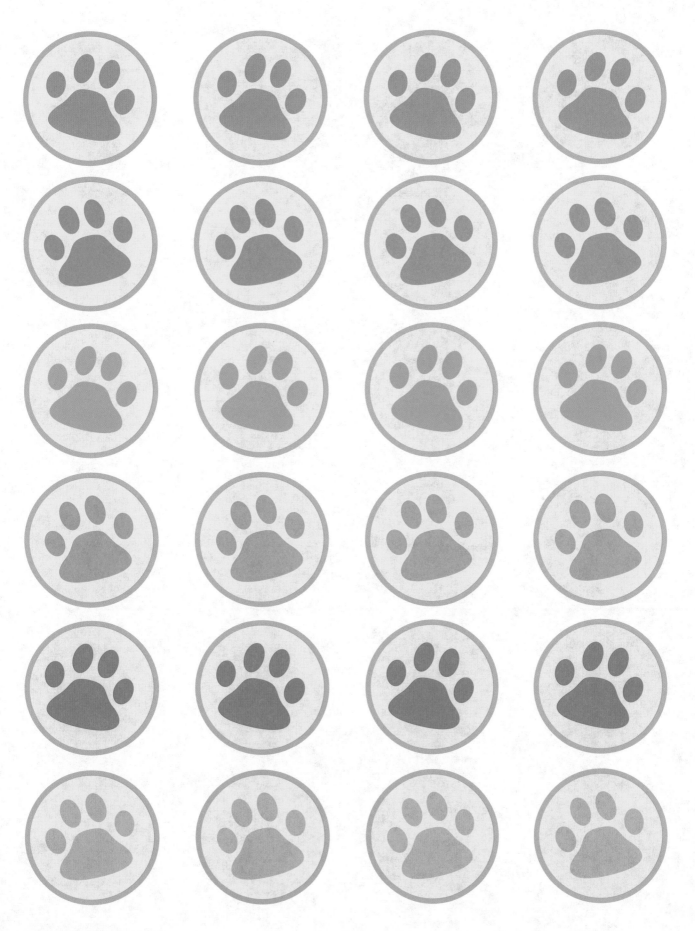

Cowboy in the Cornfield

Ending Sounds

Objective: To identify ending sounds of pictures and match them to appropriate consonant letters.

Preparation

1. Assemble and laminate the Cowboy in the Cornfield Game Board (pages 120 and 121).

2. Laminate and cut out the Cowboy in the Cornfield Ending Sound Picture Cards (pages 123, 125, and 127).

3. Laminate and cut out the Corn Cover Ups (page 129).

4. Laminate the Cowboy in the Cornfield Directions Card (page 117).

5. Store the Cowboy in the Cornfield Ending Sound Picture Cards and Corn Cover Ups in a resealable snack bag. Label the bag with the game name label (page 175).

6. See page 176 for the correct picture card names.

Cowboy in the Cornfield Directions

Materials

- Cowboy in the Cornfield Game Board
- Cowboy in the Cornfield Ending Sound Picture Cards
- Corn Cover Ups

How to Play the Game

2–4 players

1. Shuffle the ending sound picture cards and place them facedown beside the Cowboy in the Cornfield Game Board.

2. Divide the Corn Cover Ups among the players.

3. Take turns drawing an ending sound picture card and covering the matching consonant letter on the game board with a cover up.

4. Continue taking turns until all the consonant letters on the Cowboy in the Cornfield Game Board have been covered.

Ending Sound Picture Cards

Cowboy
in the
Cornfield

Cowboy
in the
Cornfield

Cowboy
in the
Cornfield

Cowboy
in the
Cornfield

Cowboy
in the
Cornfield

#3120 Full-Color Reading Games Pre K–K

Ending Sound Picture Cards

Cowboy
in the
Cornfield

Cowboy
in the
Cornfield

Cowboy
in the
Cornfield

Cowboy
in the
Cornfield

Cowboy
in the
Cornfield

Ending Sound Picture Cards

Cowboy in the Cornfield

Cowboy in the Cornfield

Cowboy in the Cornfield

Cowboy in the Cornfield

Cowboy in the Cornfield

Cowboy in the Cornfield

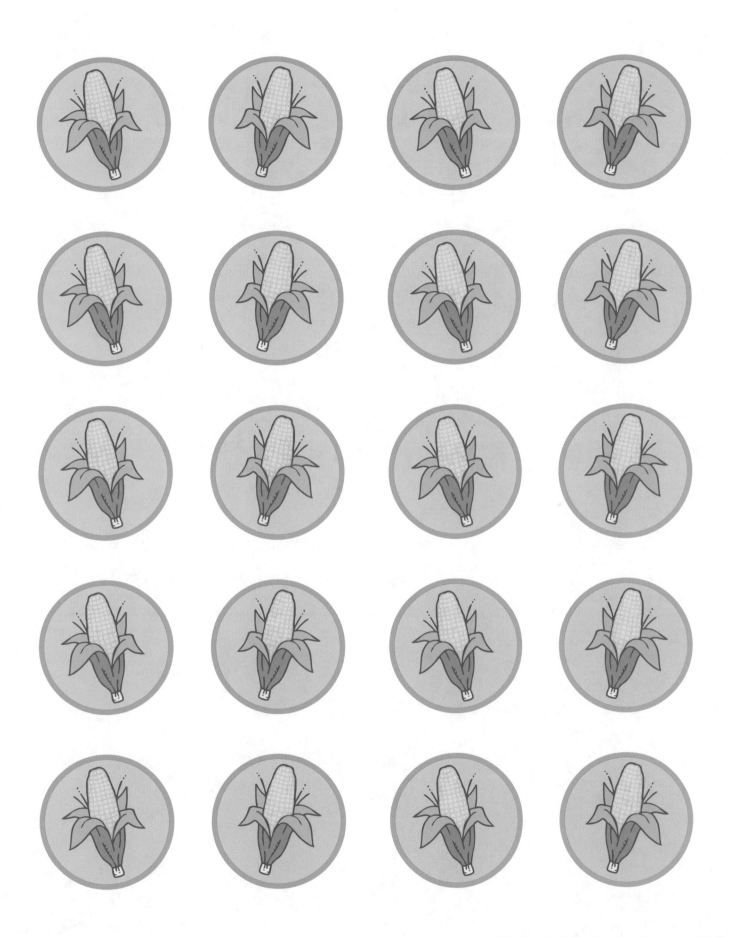

Hay Rack Ride

Ending Sounds

Objective: To identify ending sounds of pictures and match them to appropriate consonant letters.

Preparation

1. Assemble and laminate the Hay Rack Ride Game Board (pages 134 and 135).

2. Laminate and cut out the Hay Rack Ride Ending Sound Picture Cards (pages 137, 139, and 141).

3. Laminate and cut out the Hat Cover Ups (page 143).

4. Laminate the Hay Rack Ride Directions Card (page 131).

5. Store the Hay Rack Ride Ending Sound Picture Cards and Hat Cover Ups in a resealable snack bag. Label the bag with the game name label (page 175).

6. See page 176 for the correct picture card names.

Hay Rack Ride Directions

Materials

- Hay Rack Ride Game Board
- Hay Rack Ride Ending Sound Picture Cards
- Hat Cover Ups

How to Play the Game

2–4 players

1. Shuffle the ending sound picture cards and place them facedown beside the Hay Rack Ride Game Board.

2. Divide the Hat Cover Ups among the players.

3. Take turns drawing an ending sound picture card and covering the matching consonant letter on the game board with a cover up.

4. Continue taking turns until all the consonant letters on the Hay Rack Ride Game Board have been covered.

Ending Sound Picture Cards

Hay Rack Ride

Hay Rack Ride

Hay Rack Ride

Hay Rack Ride

Hay Rack Ride

Ending Sound Picture Cards

Hay Rack
Ride

Hay Rack
Ride

Hay Rack
Ride

Hay Rack
Ride

Hay Rack

Ride

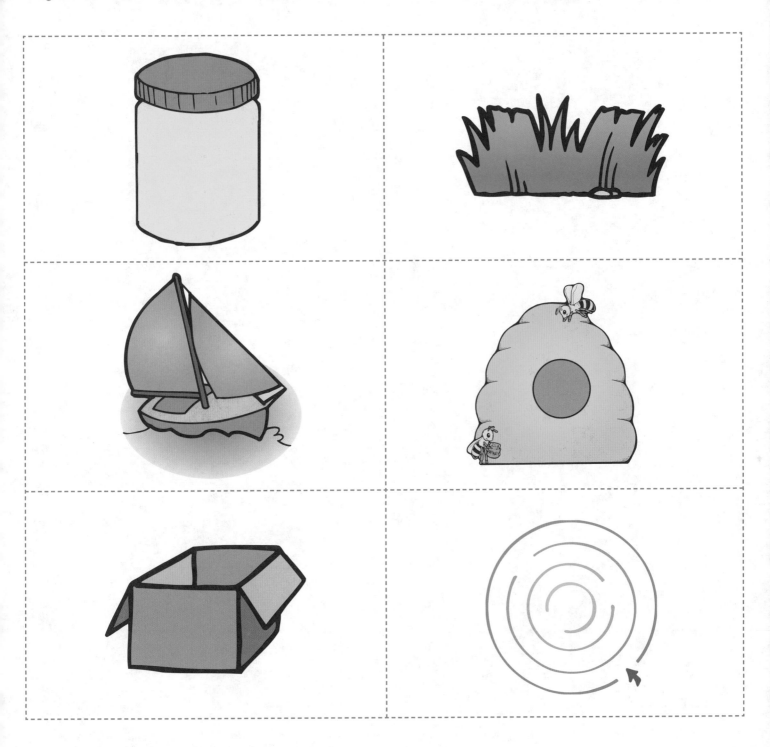

Ending Sound Picture Cards

Hay Rack
Ride

Hay Rack
Ride

Hay Rack
Ride

Hay Rack
Ride

Hay Rack
Ride

Hay Rack
Ride

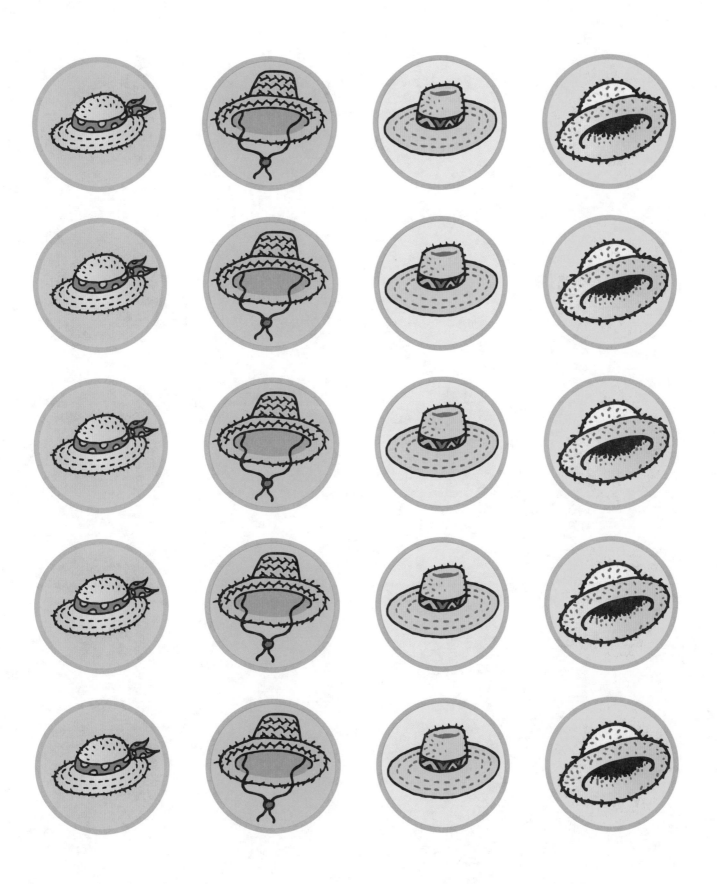

Barnyard Buddies

Ending Sounds

Objective: To identify ending sounds of pictures and match them to appropriate consonant letters.

Preparation

1. Assemble and laminate the Barnyard Buddies Game Board (pages 148 and 149).

2. Laminate and cut out the Barnyard Buddies Ending Sound Picture Cards (pages 151, 153, and 155).

3. Laminate and cut out the Farm Animal Cover Ups (page 157).

4. Laminate the Barnyard Buddies Directions Card (page 145).

5. Store the Barnyard Buddies Ending Sound Picture Cards and Farm Animal Cover Ups in a resealable snack bag. Label the bag with the game name label (page 175).

6. See page 176 for the correct picture card names.

Barnyard Buddies Directions

Materials

- Barnyard Buddies Game Board
- Barnyard Buddies Ending Sound Picture Cards
- Farm Animal Cover Ups

How to Play the Game

2–4 players

1. Shuffle the ending sound picture cards and place them facedown beside the Barnyard Buddies Game Board.

2. Divide the Farm Animal Cover Ups among the players.

3. Take turns drawing an ending sound picture card and covering the matching consonant letter on the game board with a cover up.

4. Continue taking turns until all the consonant letters on the Barnyard Buddies Game Board have been covered.

#3120 Full-Color Reading Games Pre K–K

BARNYARD BUDDIES

z

s

m

g

d

x

l

f

c

p

n

Ending Sound Picture Cards

Barnyard
Buddies

Barnyard
Buddies

Barnyard
Buddies

Barnyard
Buddies

Barnyard
Buddies

Ending Sound Picture Cards

Barnyard
Buddies

Barnyard
Buddies

Barnyard
Buddies

Barnyard
Buddies

Barnyard
Buddies

Ending Sound Picture Cards

Barnyard
Buddies

Barnyard
Buddies

Barnyard
Buddies

Barnyard
Buddies

Barnyard
Buddies

Barnyard
Buddies

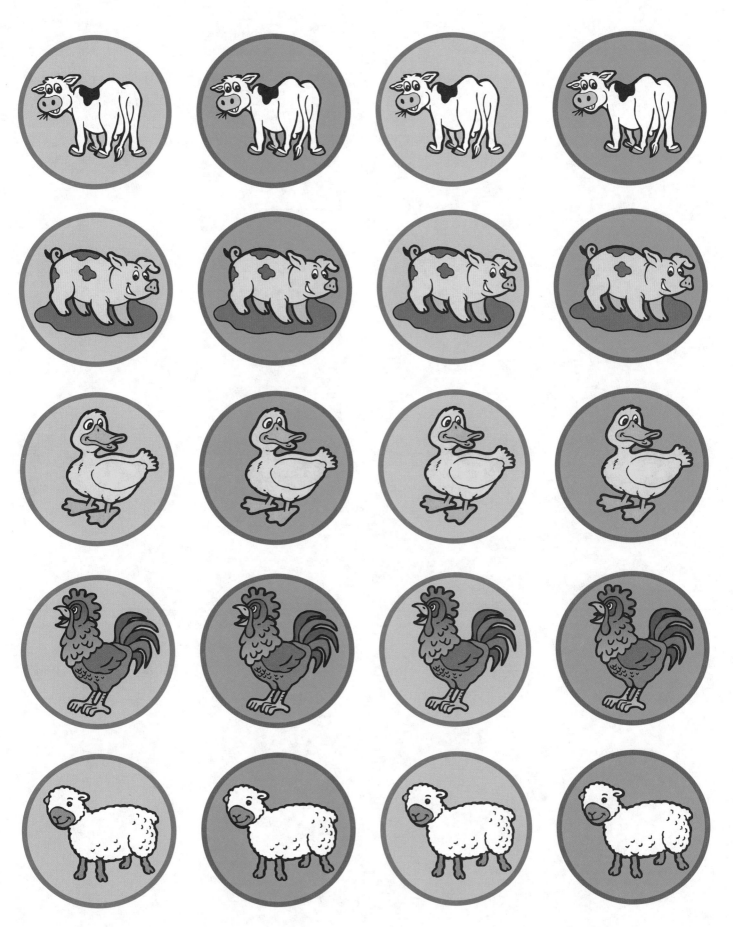

Curly the Cow

Ending Sounds

Objective: To identify ending sounds of pictures and match them to appropriate consonant letters.

Preparation

1. Assemble and laminate the Curly the Cow Game Board (pages 162 and 163).

2. Laminate and cut out the Curly the Cow Ending Sound Picture Cards (pages 165, 167, and 169).

3. Laminate and cut out the Spot Cover Ups (page 171).

4. Laminate the Curly the Cow Directions Card (page 159).

5. Store the Curly the Cow Ending Sound Picture Cards and Spot Cover Ups in a resealable snack bag. Label the bag with the game name label (page 175).

6. See page 176 for the correct picture card names.

Curly the Cow Directions

Materials

- Curly the Cow Game Board
- Curly the Cow Ending Sound Picture Cards
- Spot Cover Ups

How to Play the Game

2–4 players

1. Shuffle the ending sound picture cards and place them facedown beside the Curly the Cow Game Board.

2. Divide the Spot Cover Ups among the players.

3. Take turns drawing an ending sound picture card and covering the matching consonant letter on the game board with a cover up.

4. Continue taking turns until all the consonant letters on the Curly the Cow Game Board have been covered.

Ending Sound Picture Cards

Curly
the
Cow

Curly
the
Cow

Curly
the
Cow

Curly
the
Cow

Curly
the
Cow

Ending Sound Picture Cards

Curly

the

Cow

Curly

the

Cow

Curly

the

Cow

Curly

the

Cow

Curly

the

Cow

168

Ending Sound Picture Cards

Curly the Cow

Curly the Cow

Curly the Cow

Curly the Cow

Curly the Cow

Curly the Cow

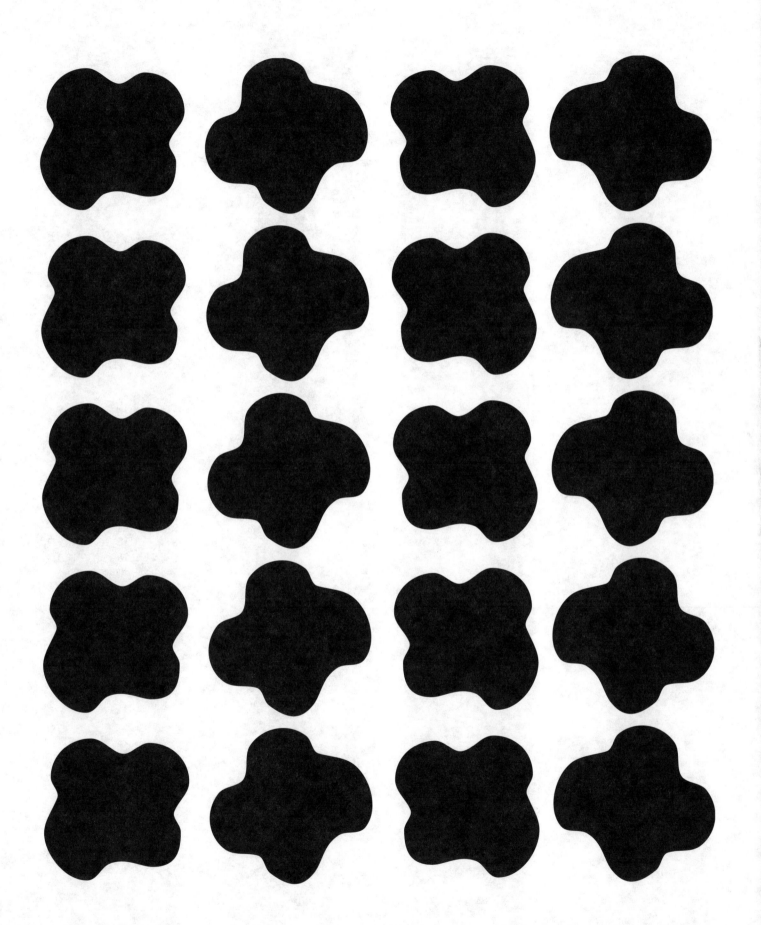

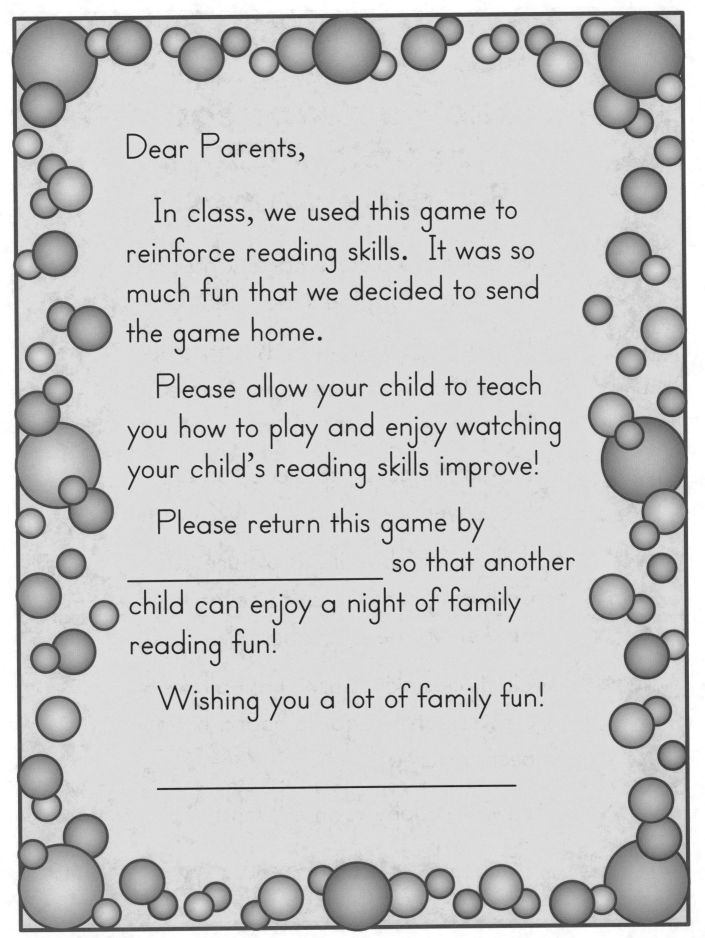

Dear Parents,

   In class, we used this game to reinforce reading skills. It was so much fun that we decided to send the game home.

   Please allow your child to teach you how to play and enjoy watching your child's reading skills improve!

   Please return this game by _____ so that another child can enjoy a night of family reading fun!

   Wishing you a lot of family fun!

   _____

Instructions for Family Fun Reading Games

❤ Remove the picture cards and cover up pieces from the snack bag.

❤ Shuffle the picture cards and place them facedown beside the game board.

❤ Divide the cover up pieces among the players.

❤ Take turns drawing a picture card and using a cover up to cover the answer on the game board.

❤ Continue taking turns until all the answers on the game board have been covered.

Have a Happy Game Night!

Game Labels

 Sammy Sea Otter

 Otto Octopus

 A Sea of Seahorses

 Whale Watching

 Flashy Fish

 Happy Hamsters

 Baby Birds

 Kitten Kingdom

 Cowboy in the Cornfield

 Hay Rack Ride

 Barnyard Buddies

 Curly the Cow

Page 67 – bed, cake, dinosaur, feather, game, hand, jar, key
Page 69 – lamp, map, nine, pumpkin, queen, rug
Page 71 – sock, ten, vest, wagon, yarn, zebra

Page 81 – ball, car, doll, fox, goat, heart, jam, kite
Page 83 – leaf, milk, nest, purse, quarter, ring
Page 85 – sun, tub, volcano, well, yogurt, zoo

Page 95 – bus, cookies, duck, fire, gas pump, hive, jeep, king
Page 97 – log, mop, nail, pie, question mark, rooster
Page 99 – six, top, vase, wolf, yo-yo, zero

Page 109 – bike (bicycle), carrots, desk, fish, gum, hose, jump rope, kangaroo
Page 111 – lock, mug, net, pen, quiet, rain
Page 113 – seal, tape, van, wave, yawn, zig zag

Page 123 – crab, picnic, road, leaf, dog
Page 125 – bike, bell, ham, corn, stamp
Page 127 – fire, gas pump, heart, wave, fox, maze

Page 137 – bib, music, bird, golf, egg
Page 139 – rake, doll, jam, fin, rope
Page 141 – jar, grass, boat, hive, box, maze

Page 151 – tub, picnic, bed, roof, frog
Page 153 – book, nail, drum, can, map
Page 155 – feather, bus, kite, cave, six, maze

Page 165 – crib, music, bride, elf, flag
Page 167 – fork, owl, vacuum, fan, trap
Page 169 – door, dress, goat, five, ax, maze